THERAPEUTIC
COLORING BOOK

Sketch Book, Notebook and Doodle Book

For Students with Learning Challenges.

Dear Teacher,

This therapeutic coloring book belongs to a student with _____.

The purpose of this book is to provide the student with a quiet activity when feelings of stress or overstimulation threaten the student's ability to cope. This book will help the student to relax and refocus.

This student's parents, doctor and/or therapist have decided to provide this student with this simple book and a set of colored pencils or markers to use in class as needed.

Please assist us tin helping this student to thrive in class by giving the student freedom to use this book as a method of pacification.

It is especially helpful for students with _____ to have the freedom to draw, doodle and take notes during "listening time" for purposes of right brain/ left brain integration. Students with _____ find it easier to focus, learn and remember when they activate the creative part of their mind.

Thank you for your understanding and cooperation. If the student's use of this resource causes a problem in your classroom please contact me, but please do not confront the student on this matter before consulting with me.

NAME:_____   Signature:_____
DATE: _____   PHONE: _____
Contact Information: _____
Comments:_____
_____
_____

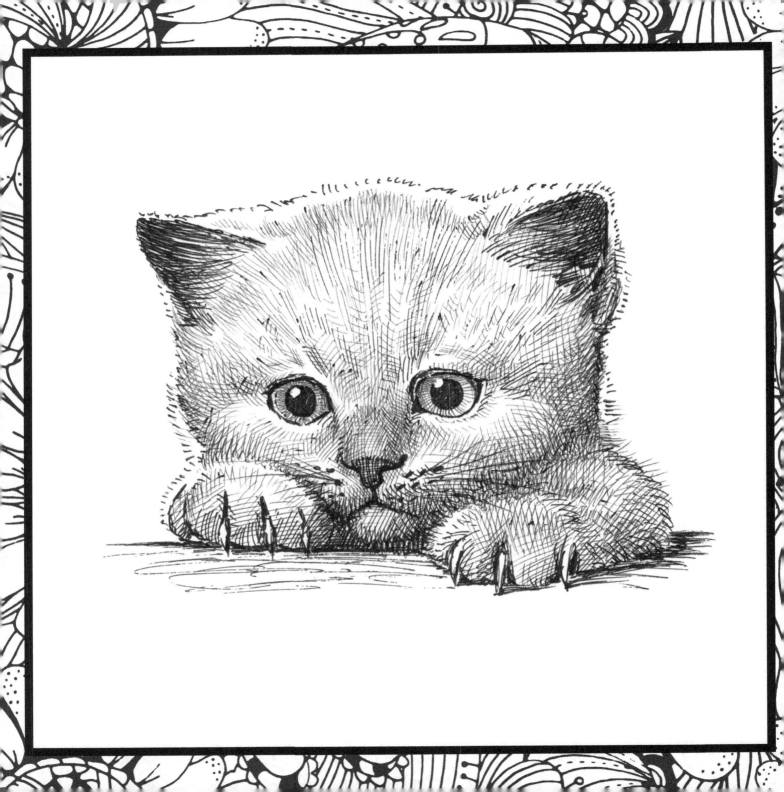

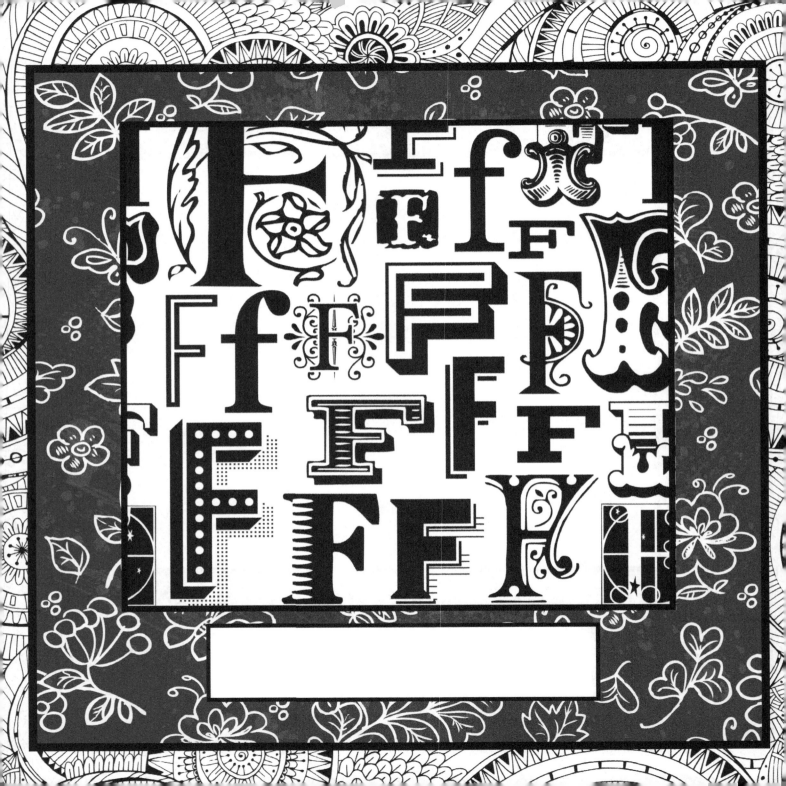

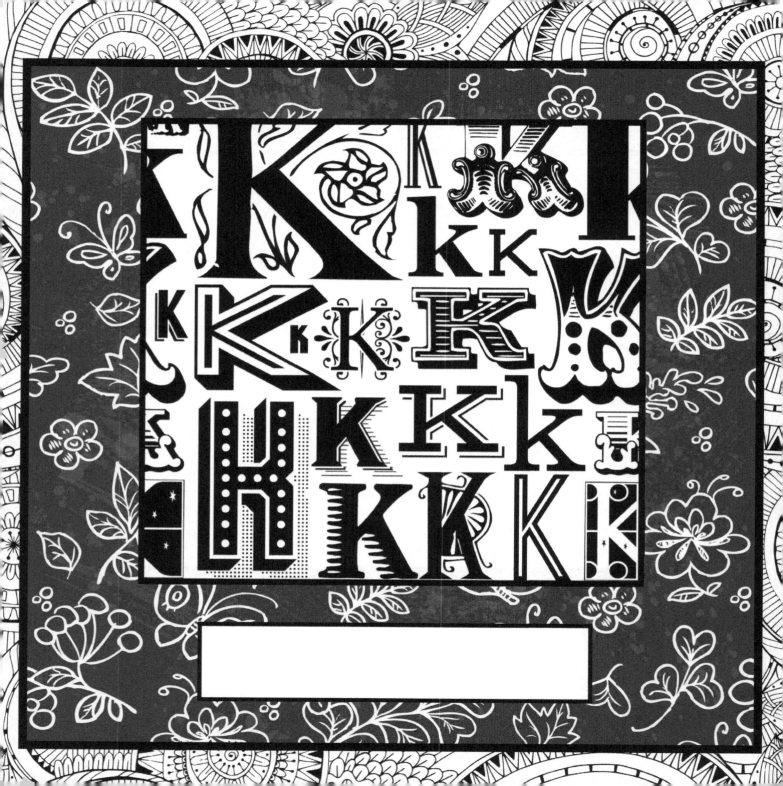

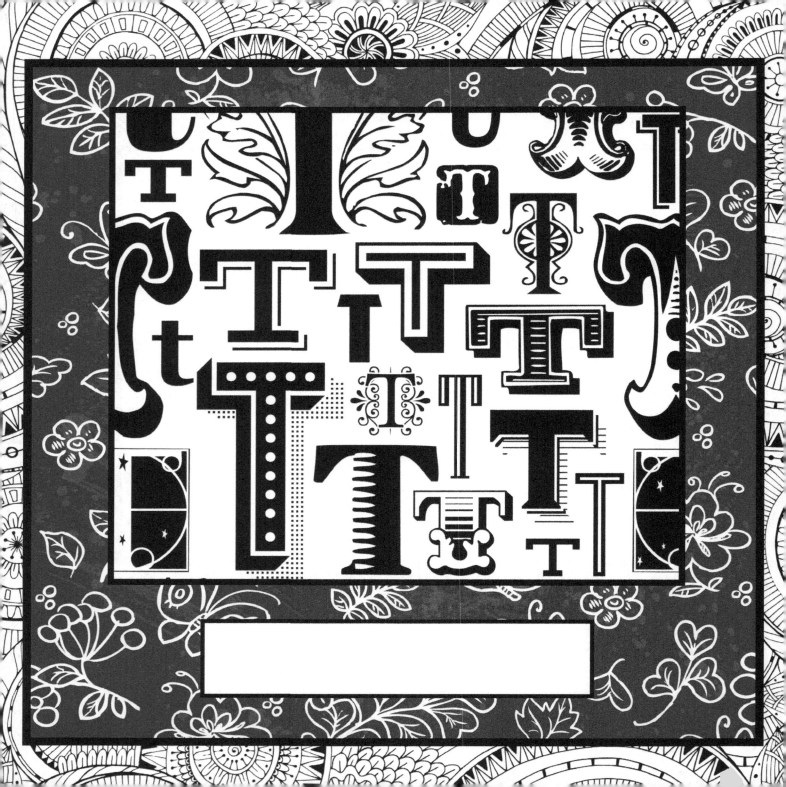

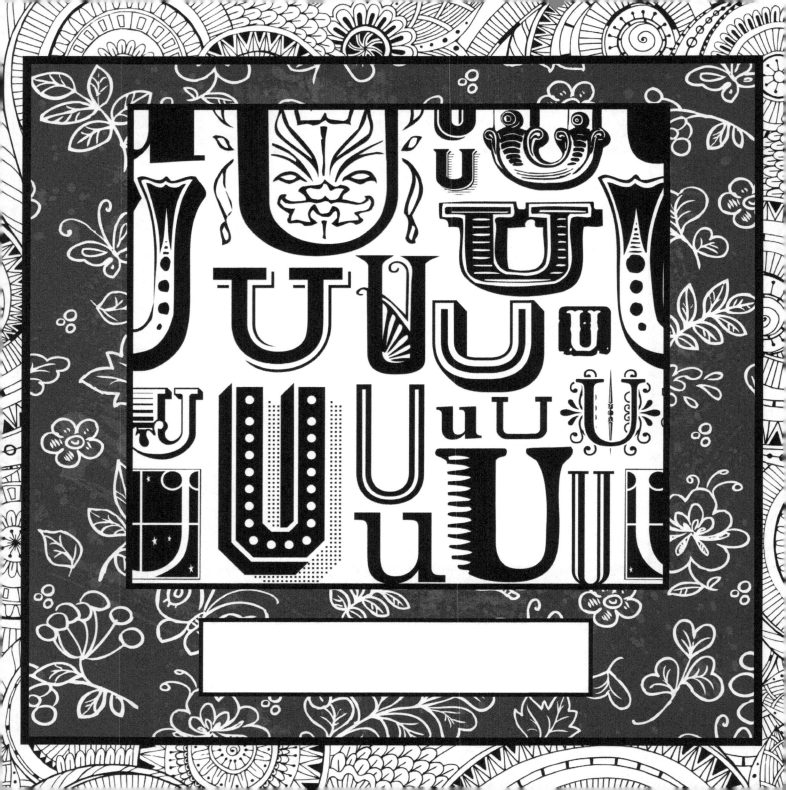

Do It Yourself
HOMESCHOOL
JOURNALS

Copyright Information

Contact Us:

The Thinking Tree LLC

617 N. Swope St. Greenfield, IN 46140. United States

317.622.8852 PHONE (Dial +1 outside of the USA) 267.712.7889 FAX

www.DyslexiaGames.com

jbrown@DyslexiaGames.com

Made in the USA
Middletown, DE
15 January 2023